TOM BRADY

A Little Golden Book® Biography

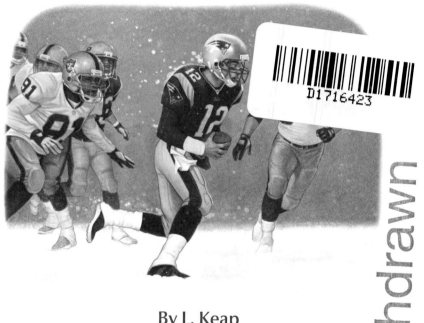

By L. Keap
Illustrated by Macky Pamintuan

g A GOLDEN BOOK • NEW YORK

Text copyright © 2024 by L. Keap
Cover art and interior illustrations copyright © 2024 by Macky Pamintuan
All rights reserved. Published in the United States by Golden Books, an imprint of
Random House Children's Books, a division of Penguin Random House LLC, 1745 Broadway,
New York, NY 10019. Golden Books, A Golden Book, A Little Golden Book, the G colophon,
and the distinctive gold spine are registered trademarks of Penguin Random House LLC.
rhcbooks.com
Educators and librarians, for a variety of teaching tools, visit us at RHTeachersLibrarians.com
Library of Congress Control Number: 2023938988
ISBN 978-0-593-65215-2 (trade) — ISBN 978-0-593-65216-9 (ebook)
Printed in the United States of America
10 9 8 7 6 5 4 3 2 1

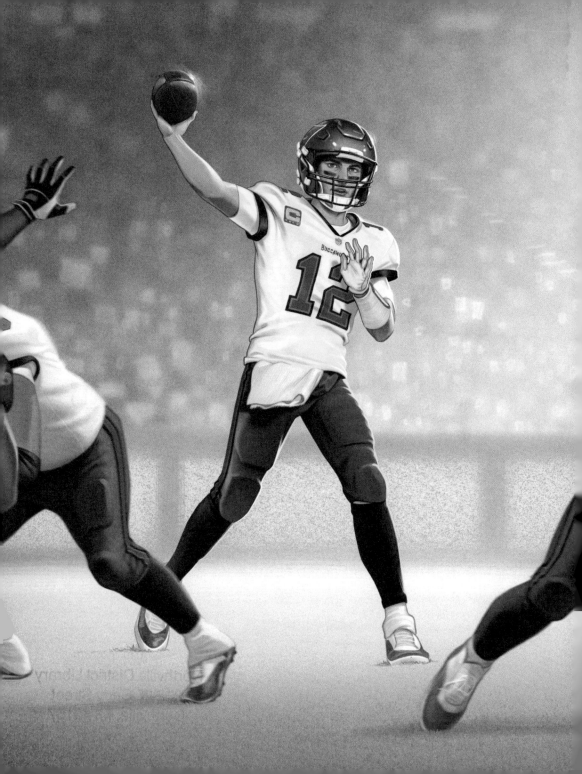

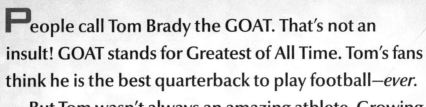

People call Tom Brady the GOAT. That's not an insult! GOAT stands for Greatest of All Time. Tom's fans think he is the best quarterback to play football—*ever*.

But Tom wasn't always an amazing athlete. Growing up, he wasn't even the best athlete in his family!

Thomas Edward Patrick Brady Jr. was born in San Mateo, California, on August 3, 1977.

Tom's three older sisters all played high school sports. Maureen and Nancy were ace softball pitchers, and Julie was a soccer star.

Tom made the football team his freshman year in high school—and mostly sat on the sidelines.

The problem? Tom had a good throwing arm. But his coach said his feet were "slow as molasses."

Not for long, Tom decided.

Tom painted five dots on the floor of his garage. He practiced stepping from dot to dot, moving his feet faster and faster. Tom repeated the Five-Dot Drill every day, sometimes late into the night.

His hard work paid off. The next year, Tom was named the quarterback of the junior varsity team! He became the varsity quarterback the year after that.

The quarterback is the leader. He handles the football when the team is trying to score.

Should he pass the ball? Run it to the end zone? The quarterback has just seconds to decide. Meanwhile, the other team is rushing to tackle him!

Tom learned to make quick, smart decisions. He played so well in high school that he won a scholarship to play football at the University of Michigan.

Tom graduated college in 1999. He was sure he knew what came next.

He would play professional football in the National Football League!

Every year, NFL teams choose new players. They announce the players' names on TV. Tom hoped his name would be one of the first ones called in 2000.

Instead, Tom heard name after name. Ten names. Twenty names. A *hundred* names! He did *not* hear "Tom Brady."

Didn't anyone want him?

Finally, the New England Patriots chose Tom—as the 199th pick!

The Patriots already had a star quarterback, Drew Bledsoe. Tom would be Drew's backup. Tom was on the sidelines . . . again.

That didn't slow him down. Tom trained every day. He lifted weights to get stronger. He memorized the team playbook.

Then, in 2001, Drew got badly hurt and couldn't play. The Patriots' coach, Bill Belichick, asked Tom if he was ready to step in.

"YES!" Tom said.

"NO!" groaned the team's fans.

It was only Tom's second season—he was practically a rookie! Did he even know what he was doing?

On September 30, 2001, Tom ran onto the field for his first game as the Patriots' starting quarterback. He felt calm and confident. The fans didn't feel the same way.

Tom quickly changed their minds! He led the team to a stunning victory over the Indianapolis Colts, 44–13.

With Tom on the field, the Patriots *kept* winning.
They won eleven of their next fourteen games—even
one during a huge snowstorm!

They made it all the way to the Super Bowl—
the biggest game in football!

The Patriots had never won a Super Bowl.
Could they do it with Tom?

It wouldn't be easy. The Patriots were facing the St. Louis Rams, the top-scoring team in the league.

Sure enough, the Rams took an early lead. Then Tom threw a pass to a teammate in the Rams' end zone.

TOUCHDOWN! The Patriots were on the scoreboard!

The teams battled the whole game. With less than two minutes left, the score was tied!

Tom made pass after pass. He got the football near the Rams' end zone. It was close enough for his team to kick a field goal.

If the ball went through the goalposts, the Patriots would get three points—and win the game. Tom watched the ball sail through the sky. . . .

"Unbelievable!" cried the announcers.

The Patriots had done it. They were the Super Bowl champs!

The crowd roared. Confetti rained down. Tom grinned and hugged his teammates.

Tom was named MVP—the Most Valuable
Player of the game!

It turned out Tom was just getting started. He led the Patriots to *five* more Super Bowl victories!

Tom played with the Patriots for twenty years, breaking nearly every quarterback record. Most touchdown passes. Most wins. Most Super Bowl MVP awards.

His teammates voted him team captain eighteen times in a row.

Some people began to wonder when Tom would retire. "He's getting too old to play," they grumbled. "He can't keep winning."

But Tom wasn't ready to leave football. In 2020, he moved to Florida to play for the Tampa Bay Buccaneers.

The Bucs weren't a strong team. They were coming off three losing seasons in a row. But guess what happened. . . .

That very first year, Tom took Tampa Bay to a Super Bowl win!

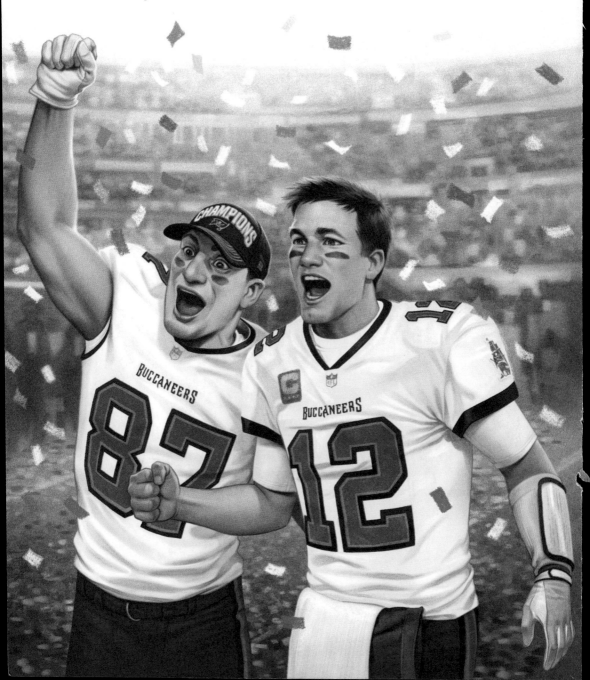

Tom stayed with the Bucs for two more seasons. In 2023, at the age of forty-five, the Greatest of All Time finally retired.

"Thank you, guys, for allowing me to live my absolute dream," he told his fans.

Tom's fans would say they're the thankful ones. For twenty-three years, they got to watch the GOAT!